DAVID LANZ Movements of the Heart

Visit David online at **DavidLanz.com**

Movements of the Heart artwork by Daniela Boifava
Vision Gate Design – **visiongate.com**

Music editing by Kathy Parsons
mainlypiano.com

Cover photo by Rosanne Olson
rosanneolson.com

ISBN 978-1-4803-6459-2

HAL•LEONARD® CORPORATION
7777 W. BLUEMOUND RD. P.O. BOX 13819 MILWAUKEE, WI 53213

In Australia Contact:
Hal Leonard Australia Pty. Ltd.
4 Lentara Court
Cheltenham, Victoria, 3192 Australia
Email: ausadmin@halleonard.com.au

Visit Hal Leonard Online at
www.halleonard.com

LOVE'S RETURN

By DAVID LANZ

Gently, with freedom

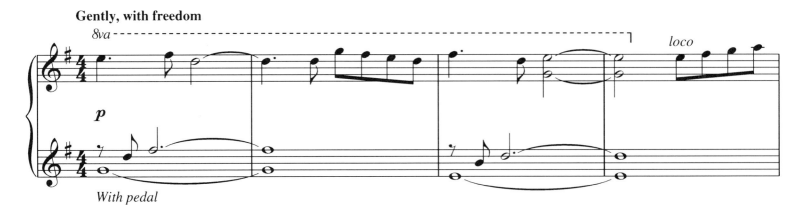

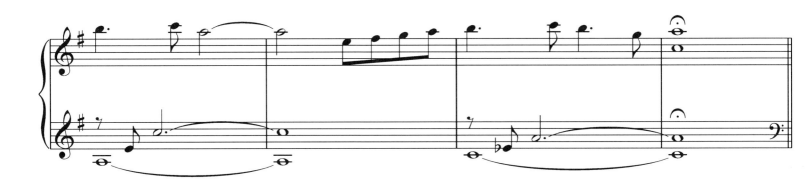

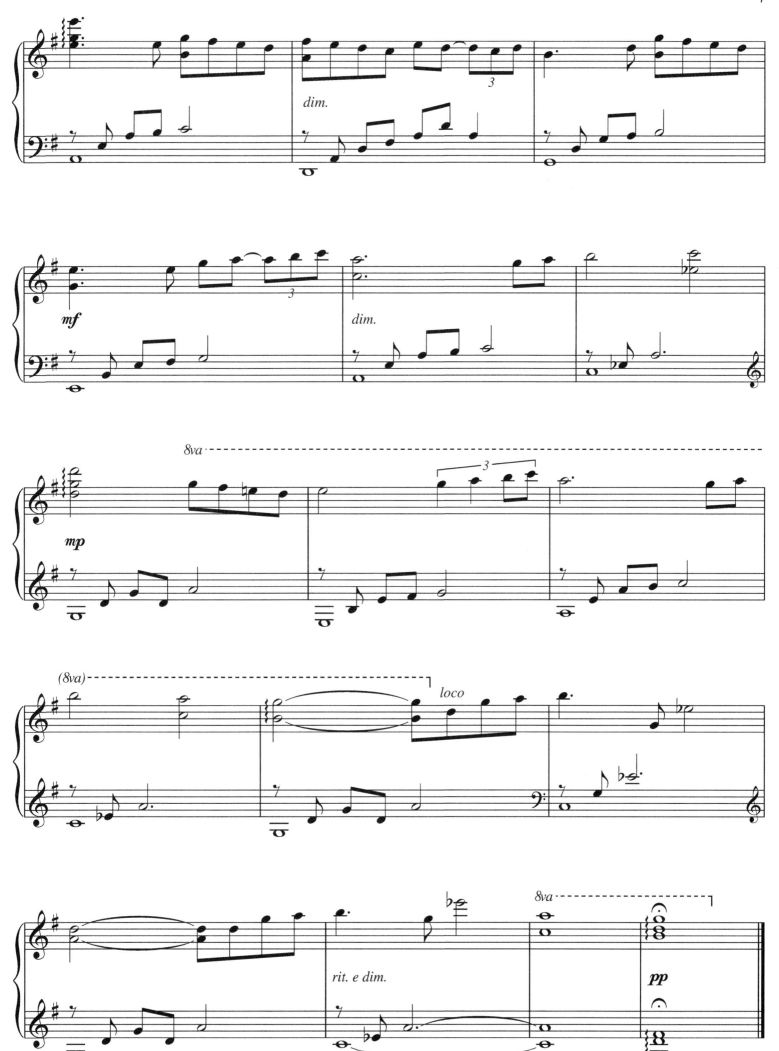

LA LUNA DELL' AMANTE

By DAVID LANZ

Gracefully flowing

With pedal

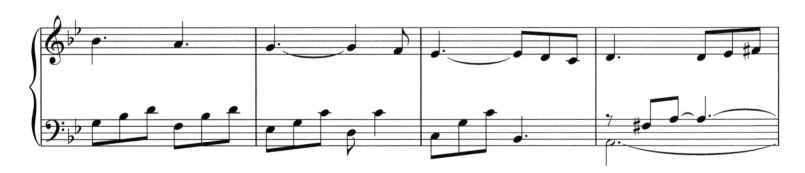

ON RAINBOW WAY

By DAVID LANZ

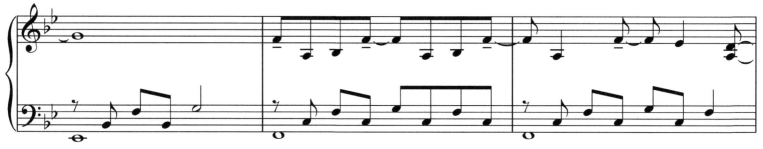

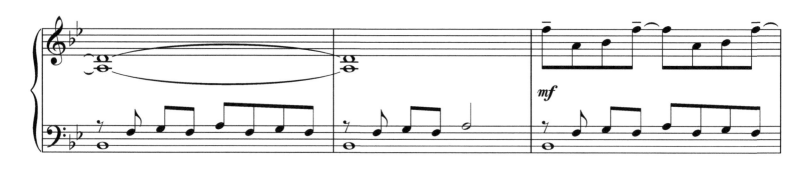

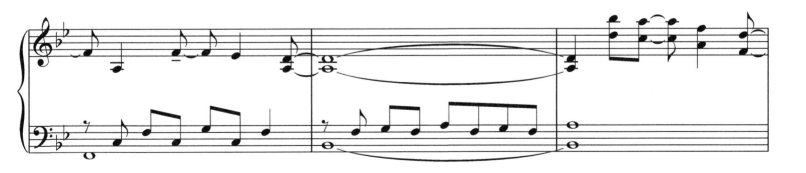

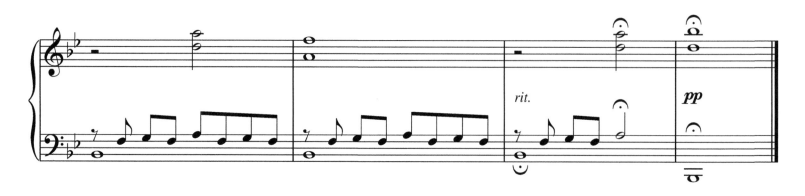

TO TOUCH THE SKY

By DAVID LANZ

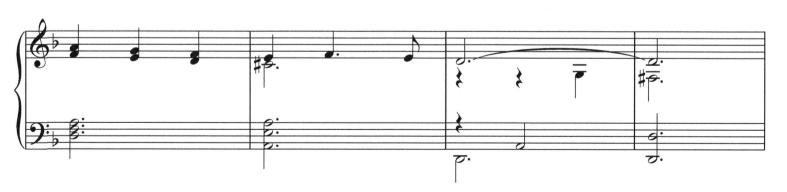

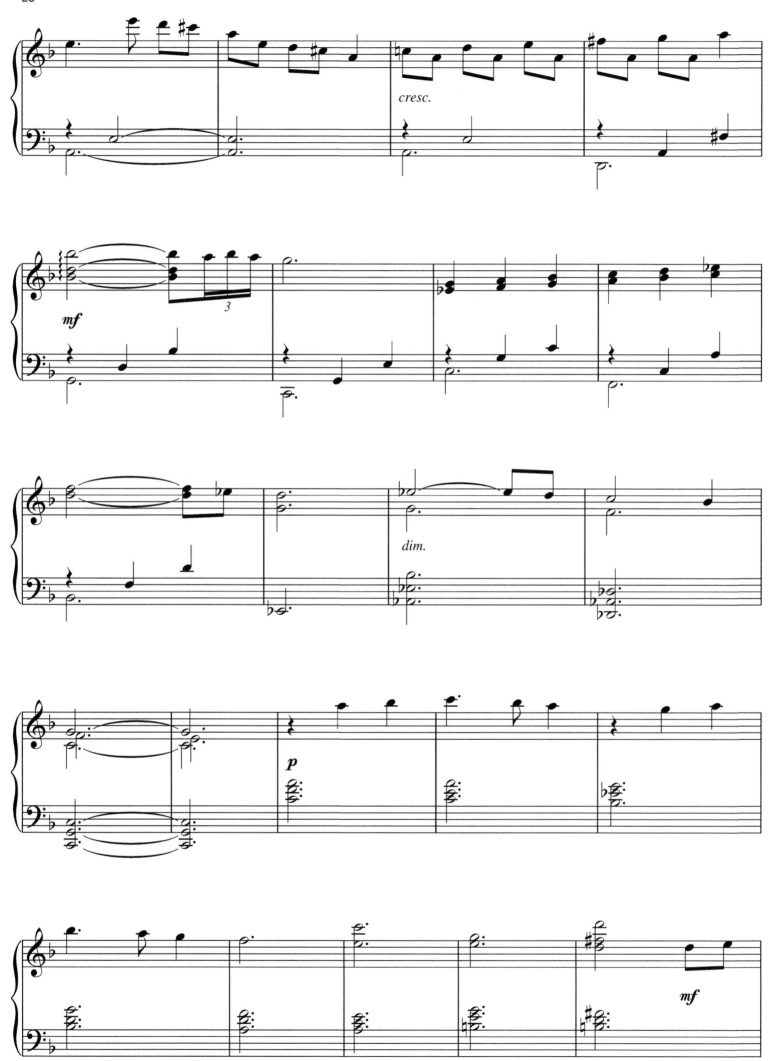

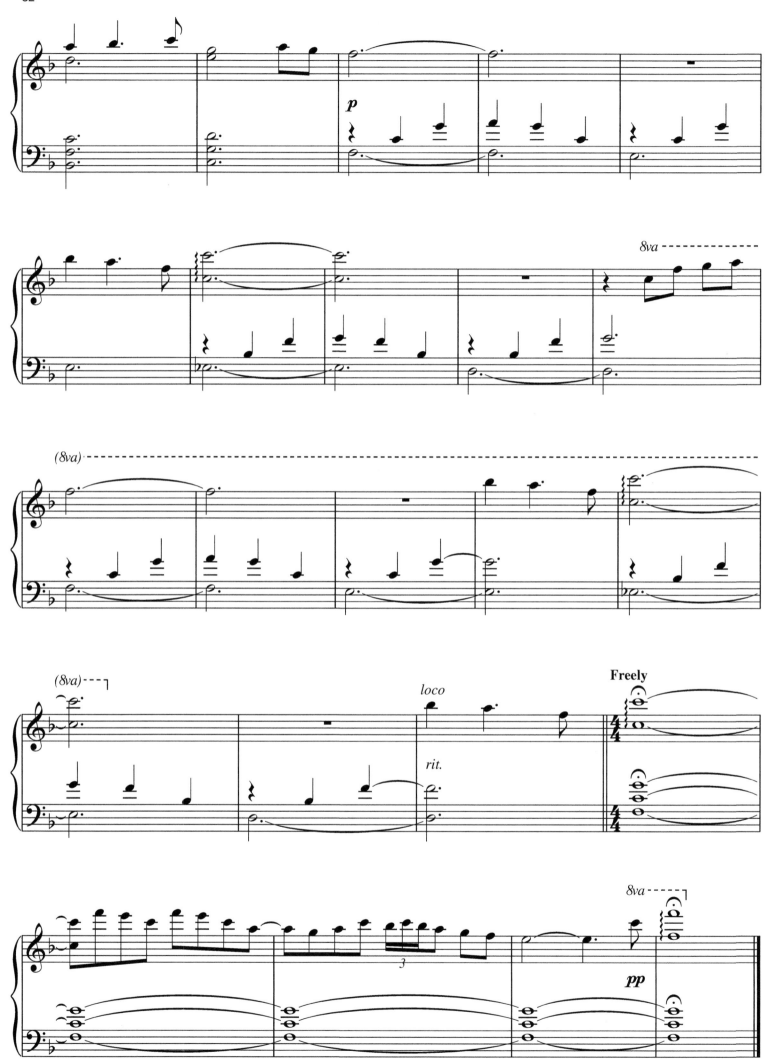

RAINLIGHT

By DAVID LANZ

Very expressively

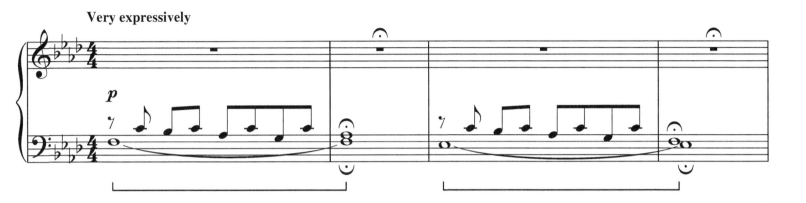

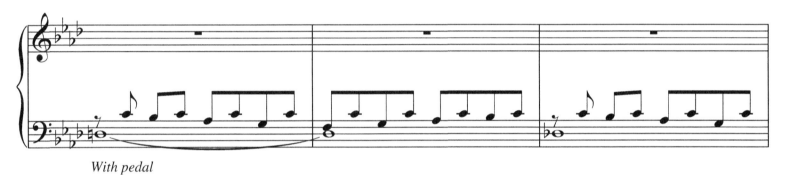

With pedal

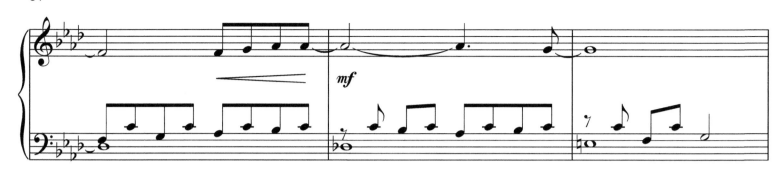

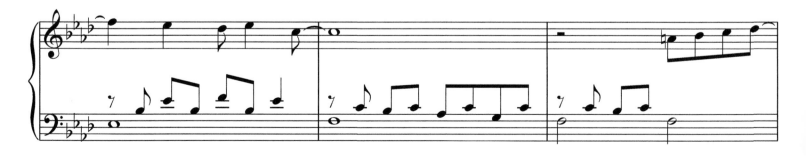

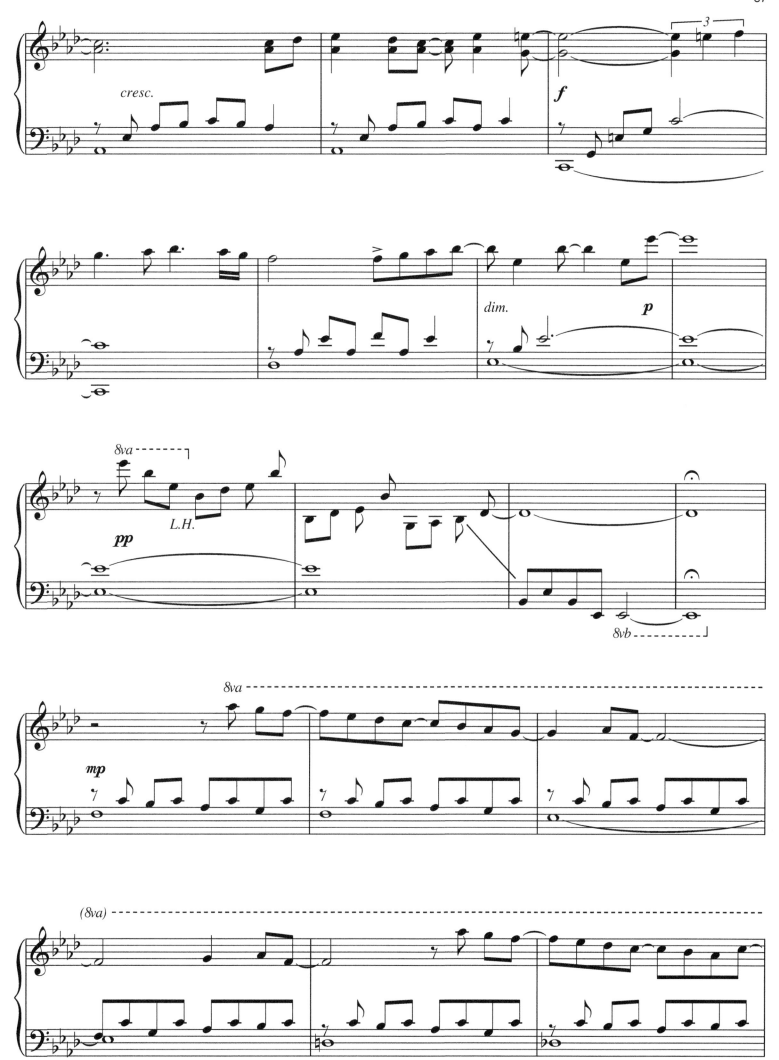

I HEAR YOU IN A SONG

By DAVID LANZ
and KRISTIN AMARIE

Lyrically and very freely

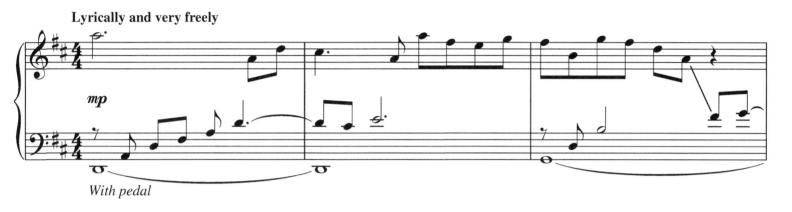

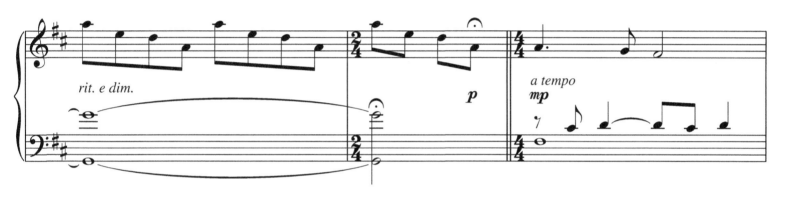

44

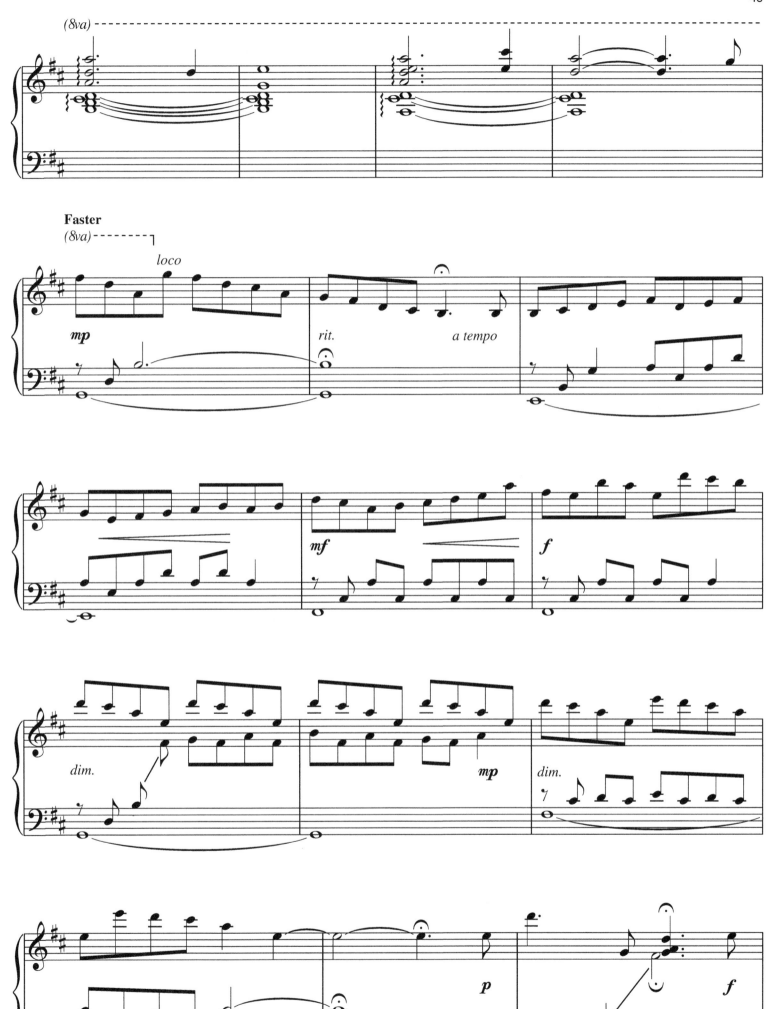

THE WAY HOME

By DAVID LANZ

Warmly

p

With pedal

A little slower

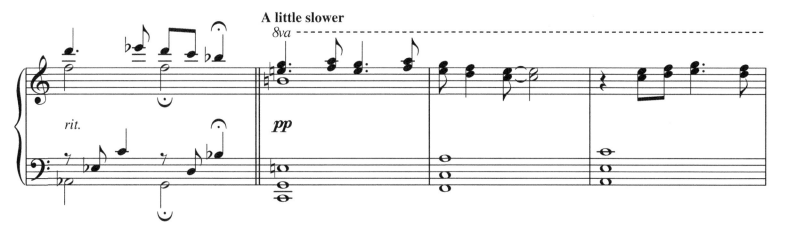

rit.

pp

Tempo I

mp

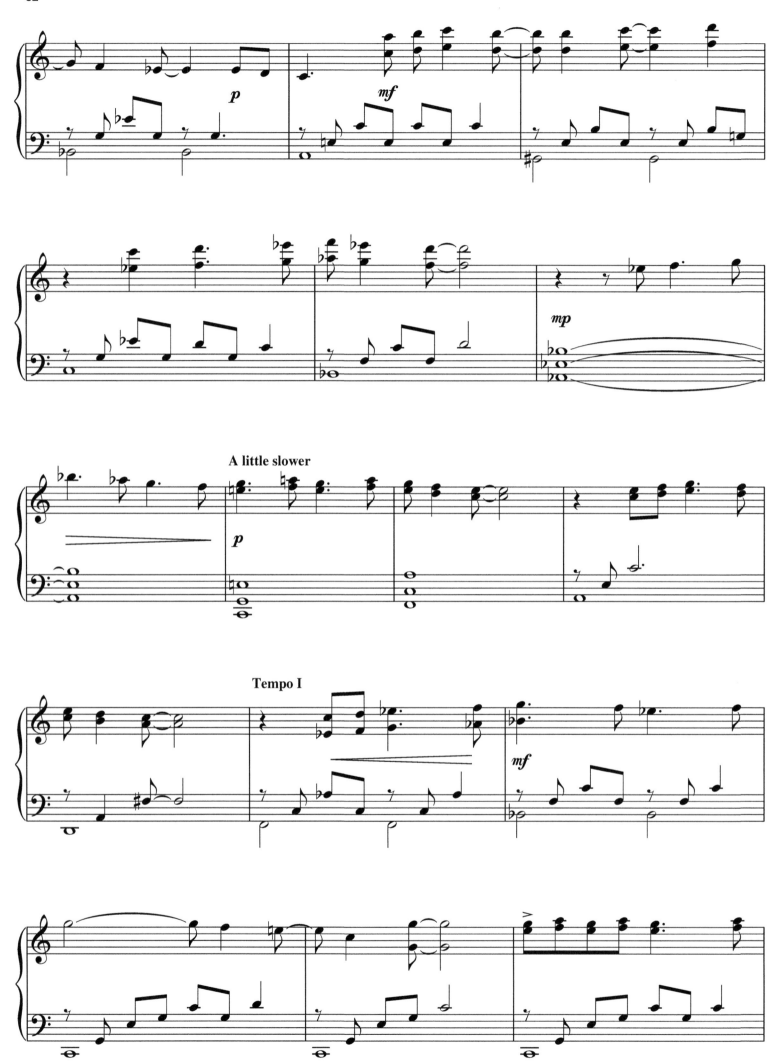

MOVEMENTS OF THE HEART

By DAVID LANZ

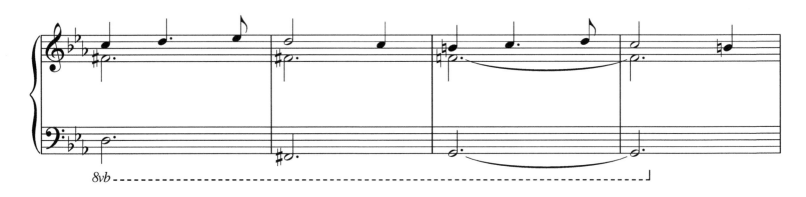

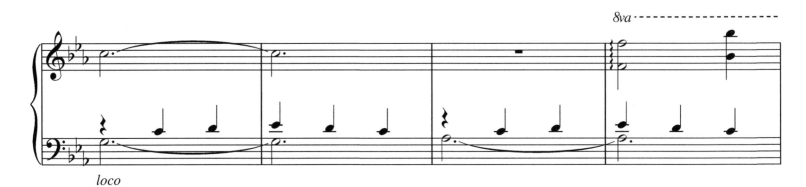

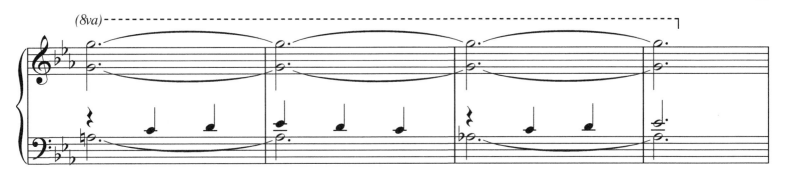

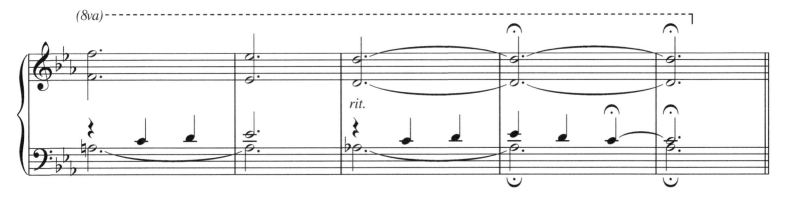

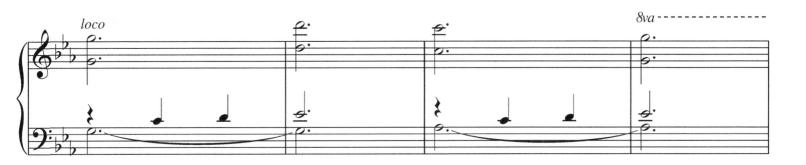

Lyrically

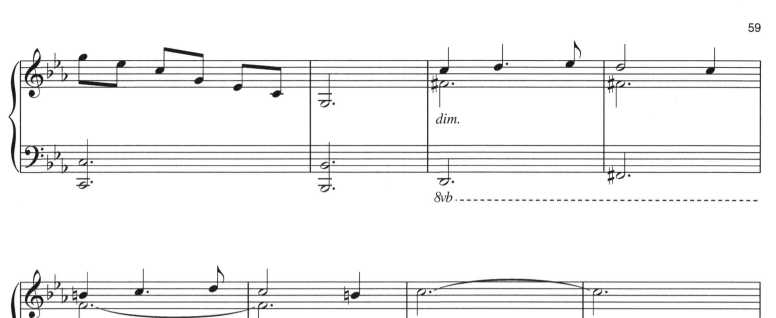

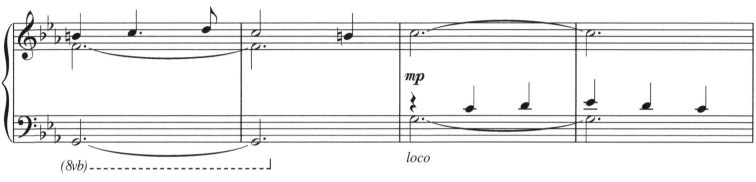

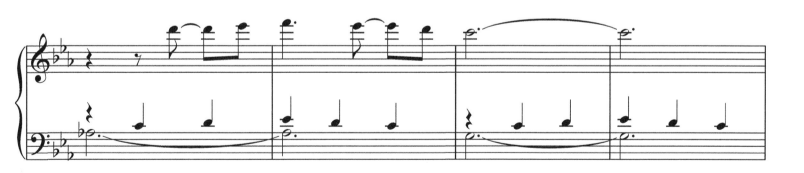

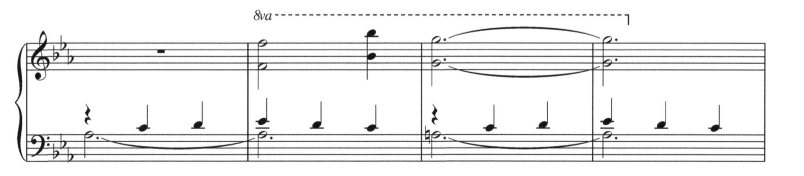

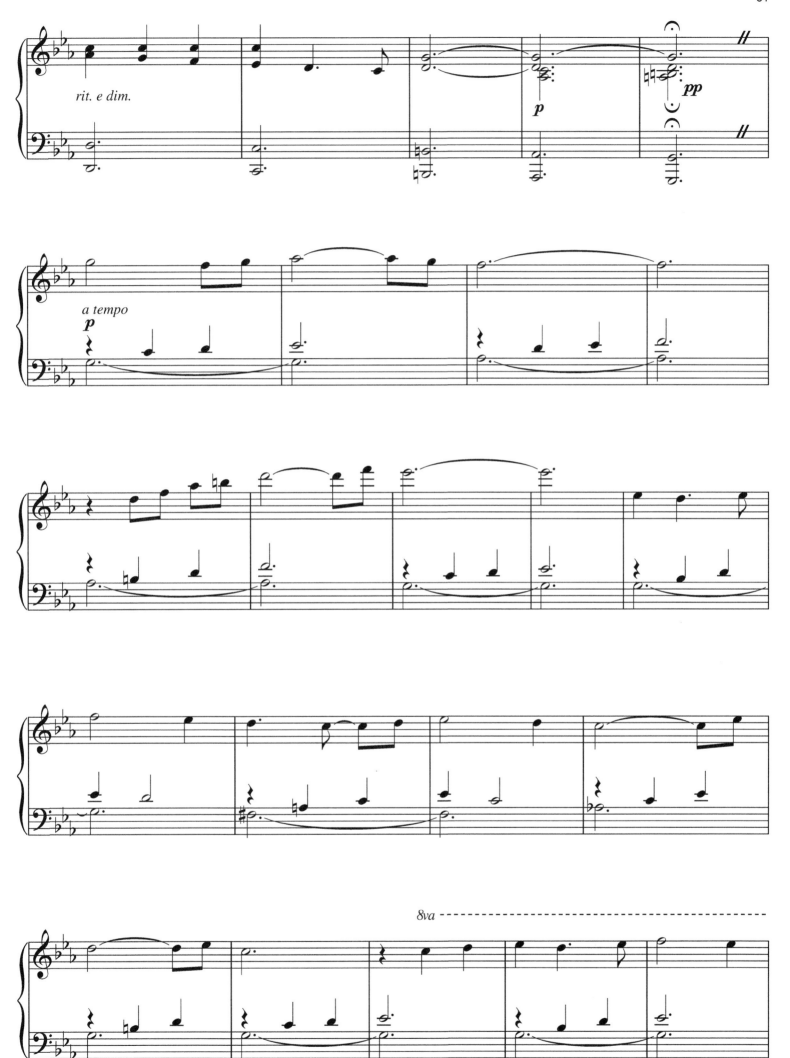

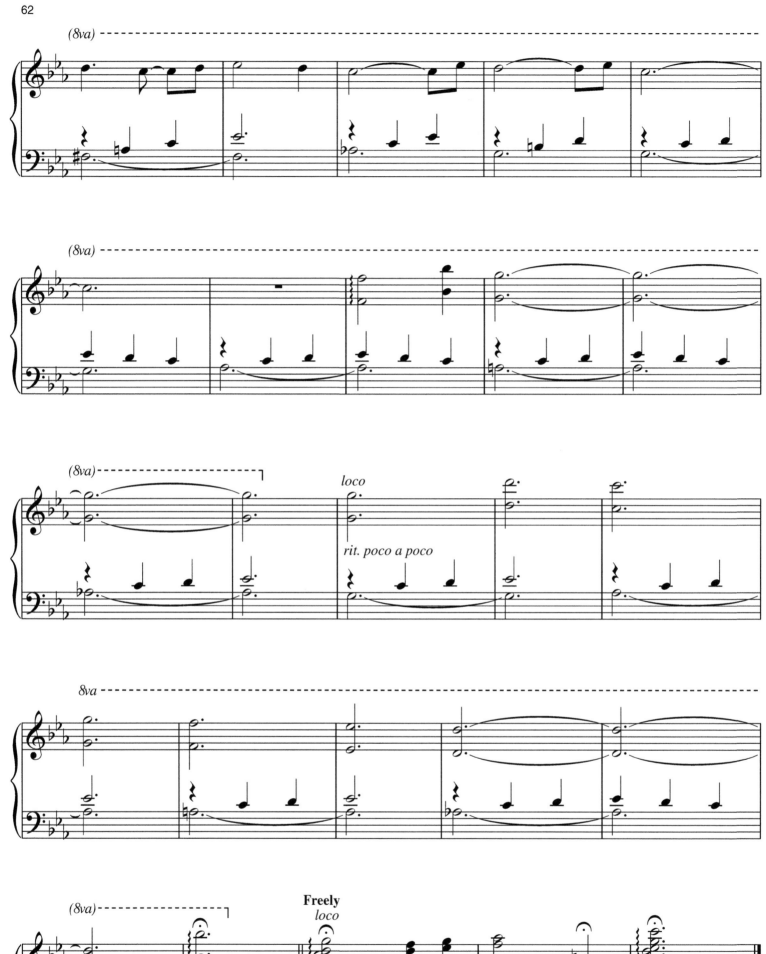

WHITE HORSE

By DAVID LANZ

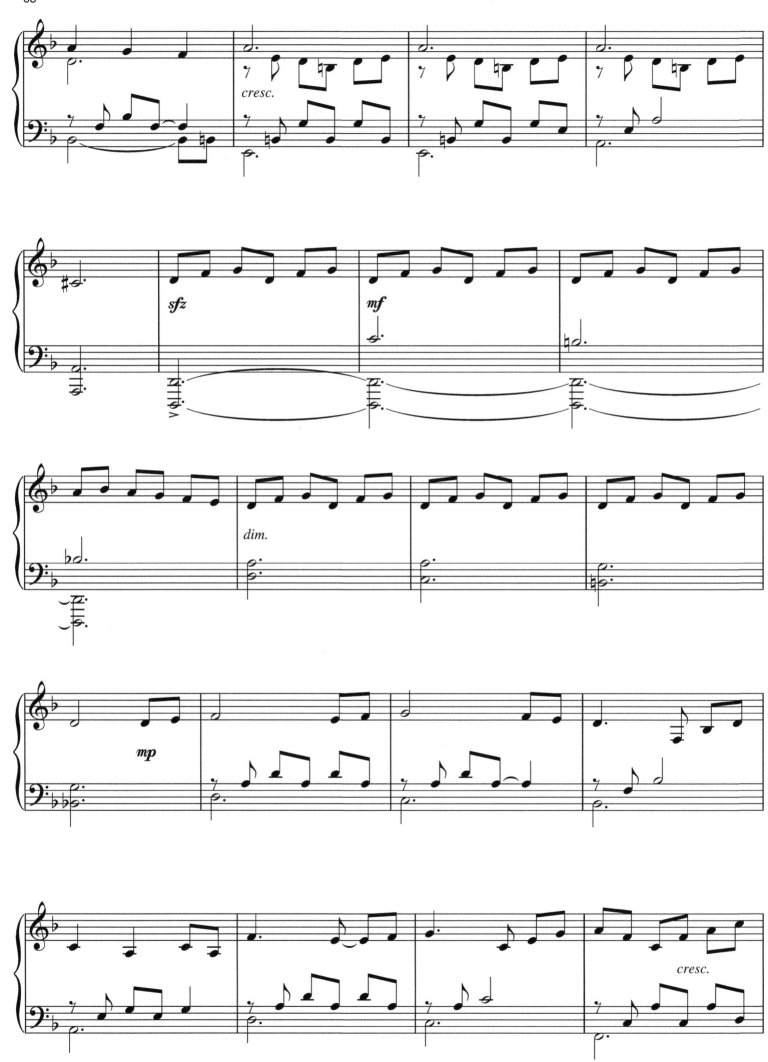

IN MOONLIGHT

By DAVID LANZ

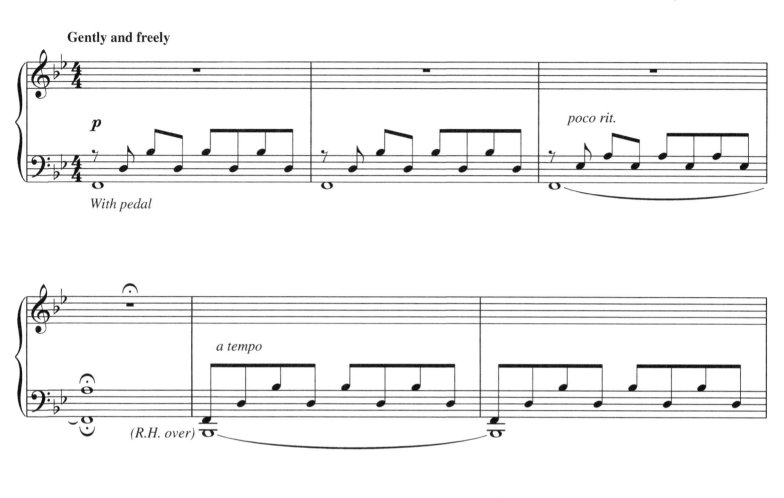

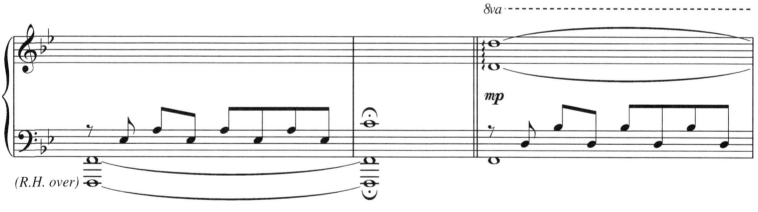

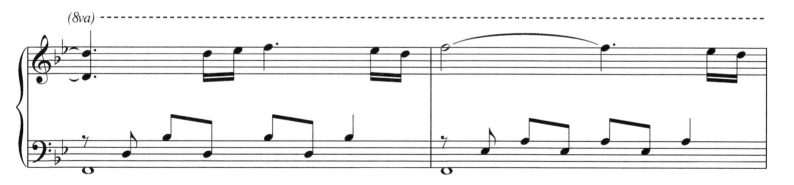

(R.H. over)

MIDNIGHT ADAGIO
(Amarie's Theme)

By DAVID LANZ

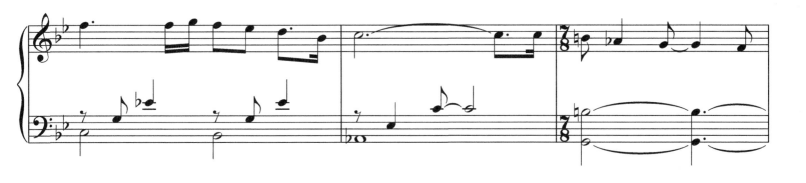

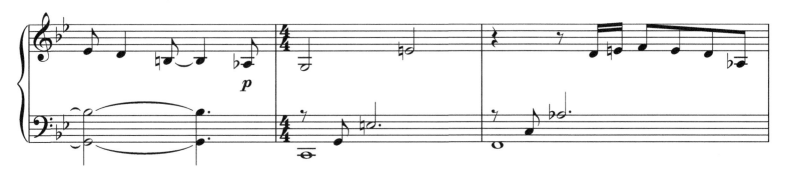

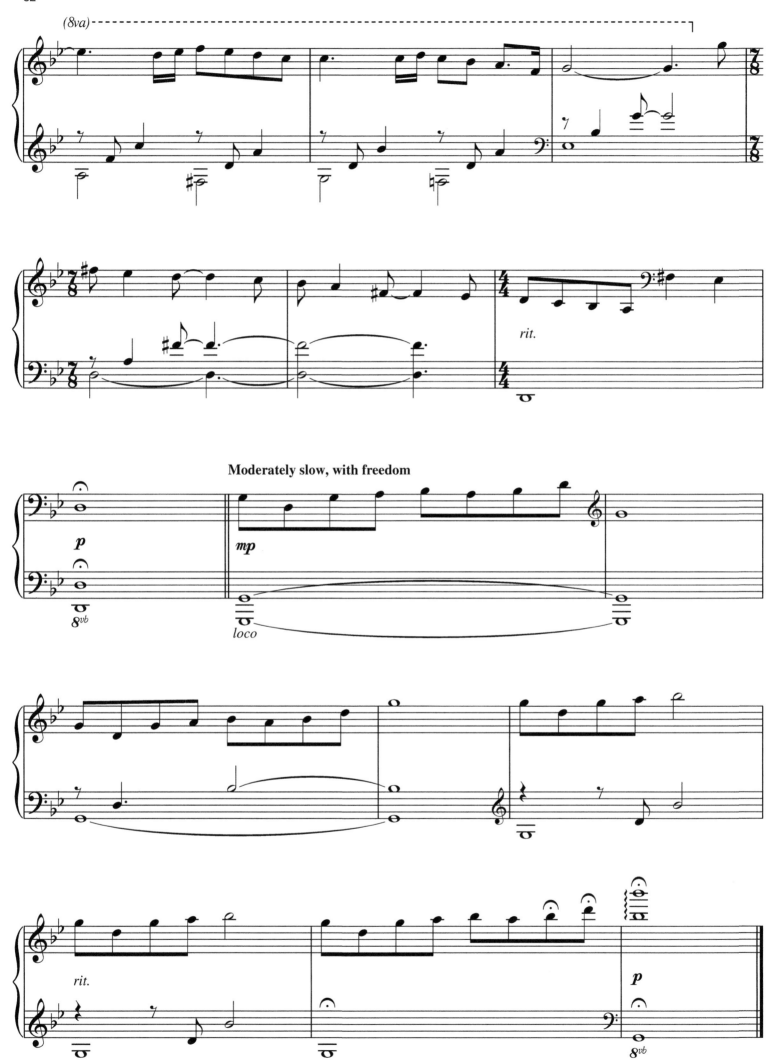

HERE AND NOW

By DAVID LANZ

Relaxed and understated

With pedal

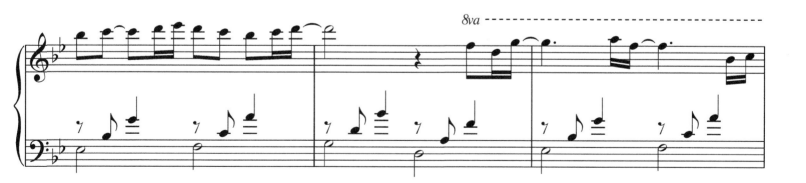

I SEE YOU IN THE STARS

By DAVID LANZ
and KRISTIN AMARIE

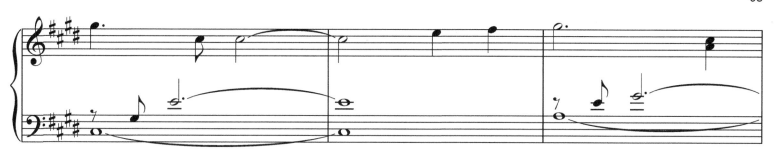

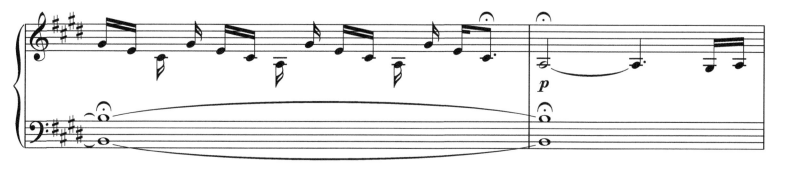

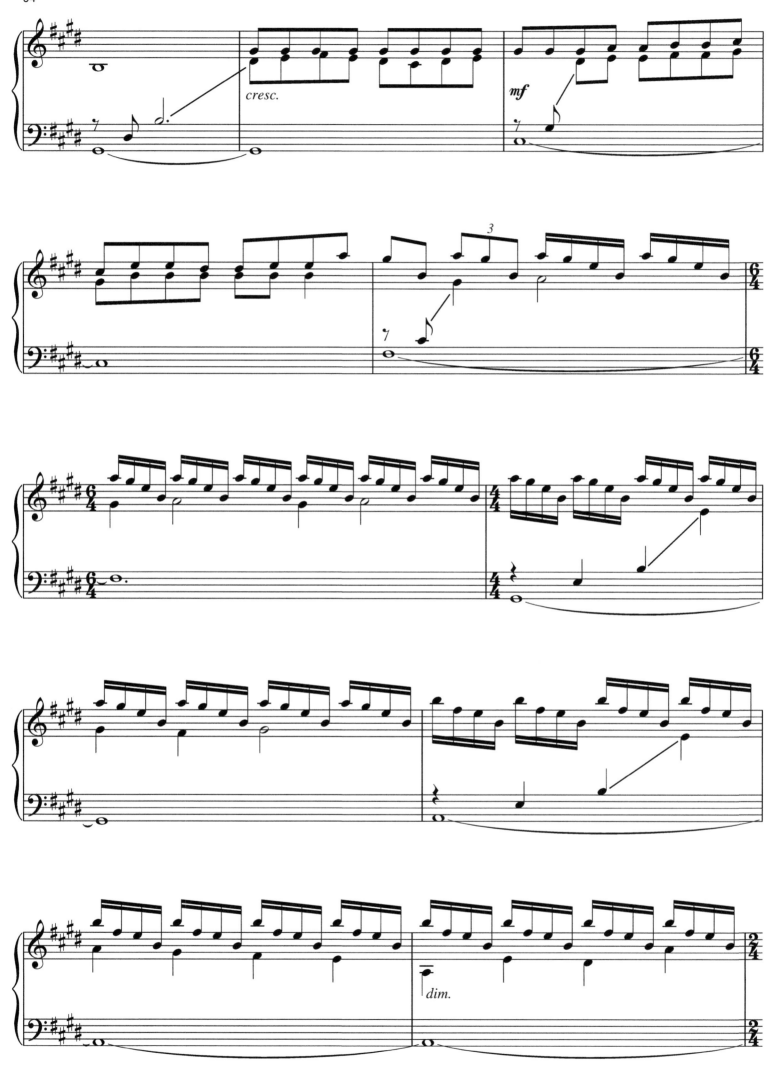